# William Shakespeare and His Times

by
Helen Sillett

Don Johnston Incorporated
Volo, Illinois

**Edited by:**

John Bergez
*Start-to-Finish Core Content Series Editor, Pacifica, California*

Alan Venable, MA
*Start-to-Finish Core Content Developmental Editor, San Francisco, California*

Gail Portnuff Venable, MS, CCC-SLP
*Speech/Language Pathologist, San Francisco, California*

Dorothy Tyack, MA
*Learning Disabilities Specialist, San Francisco, California*

Jerry Stemach, MS, CCC-SLP
*Speech/Language Pathologist, Director of Content Development, Sonoma County, California*

**Graphics and Illustrations:**

Photographs and illustrations are all created professionally
and modified to provide the best possible support for the
intended reader.
*Front cover:* Courtesy of North Wind Picture Archives ©
*Pages 21, 59:* © akg-images
*Pages 39-40:* © Shakespeare's Globe Theatre.  Photo: John Tramper
*Pages 42, 74:* © Robbie Jack/CORBIS
*Page 44:* © Hulton-Deutsch Collection/CORBIS
*Page 54:* Public Domain, courtesy of CDC/ DVBID, BZB, Entomology
and Ecology Activity, Vector Ecology & Control Laboratory, Fort Collins,
CO.  Photo: John Montenieri
*Page 55:* Public Domain, courtesy of the CDC
*Page 66:* © Viki Male, courtesy of Wikipedia
*Page 75:* © Archivo Iconografico, S.A./CORBIS
We have made every effort to trace the ownership of all copyrighted material
and to secure permission from copyright holders.  In the event of any question
arising as to the use of any material, we will be pleased to make the necessary
corrections in future printings.
All other photos © Don Johnston Incorporated and its licensors.

**Narration:**

Professional actors and actresses read the text to build
excitement and to model research-based elements of fluency:
intonation, stress, prosody, phrase groupings and rate.
The rate has been set to maximize comprehension for the reader.

**Published by:**

**Don Johnston Incorporated**
**26799 West Commerce Drive**
**Volo, IL  60073**

**800.999.4660 USA Canada**
**800.889.5242 Technical Support**
**www.donjohnston.com**

*Copyright © 2006 Start-to-Finish L.L.C. and Don Johnston Incorporated.  All rights reserved.*
*Start-to-Finish and the Don Johnston logo are registered trademarks of Don Johnston Incorporated.*
*Printed in the U.S.A.  No part of this publication may be reproduced, stored in a retrieval*
*system or transmitted in any form or by any means electronic, mechanical photocopying, recording, or otherwise.*

International Standard Book Number
ISBN-10:  1-4105-0631-2
ISBN-13:  978-1-4105-0631-3

# Table of Contents

# Introduction: A Country Boy Heads to the City

Sometime near the end of the 1500s — nobody knows when exactly — a young man arrived in London, the biggest city in England.

The young man was probably shocked when he walked through London's city gates. He had grown up in a small town with only 1500 people. London was like a different world. It was overcrowded, dirty, and full of disease. Its stinking streets were covered with human waste (urine and feces). There were pickpockets and thieves everywhere.

If he looked up, he might have seen pieces of bloody bodies hanging above him near the city walls. On London Bridge, he might have seen bloody human heads displayed on the ends of long sticks. These were the remains of people who had committed crimes against the queen.

A common sight on London Bridge
during the late 1500s

London may have been filthy and full of
disease and danger, but it was also one of the most
exciting cities in the world. Our young man
had come here hoping to find fame and fortune.

If you had seen the young man arrive,
you probably wouldn't have guessed what was
in store for him. He was just a country lad,
with no college education, but he would become
one of the greatest **playwrights** of his time.
(A playwright is a person who writes plays.)

His plays were performed before thousands of people, including the Queen of England. When he died in 1616, he was a very wealthy man.

Perhaps you've heard of this playwright. His name is William Shakespeare. You may have heard of his plays — maybe *Romeo and Juliet*, *Hamlet*, *King Lear*, *Othello*, *Macbeth*, *Julius Caesar*, or *A Midsummer Night's Dream*.

Shakespeare is even more famous today than he was in his own time. Nearly 400 years after his death, his plays are still read, performed, and studied all around the world. He is one of the greatest writers of all time.

In this book, you'll learn how a country boy who never went to college became one of the world's most important writers. You'll also learn about the dangerous, violent, and exciting times he lived in.

William Shakespeare wrote many of the world's most famous and exciting plays.

Chapter One

# Shakespeare
# in Stratford

**Questions this chapter will answer:**

• **What clues do we have about the life of young Shakespeare?**

• **What kind of schools did Shakespeare go to?**

• **What was Shakespeare's town like?**

Look into the future for a moment. Imagine that you have become a famous writer and everybody wants to know about your life. They want to know how you became such a great writer.

Today, people could look in many different places to find out about you. They could look at photographs, e-mails, or letters, or they could look at your school records. Without even thinking about it, you are leaving behind a long trail of information that somebody could use to piece together the story of your life.

People want to know all about William Shakespeare. The problem is that Shakespeare didn't leave us much information about his life.

We don't know much about William Shakespeare's life.

In this chapter, we'll take a look at the mystery of the young William Shakespeare and see what we can figure out about his early life.

## Four Clues About Young Shakespeare

Our search for the young Shakespeare starts with four small clues in documents from the time when he was young. These written records tell us a few important facts about him.

The first clue comes from a church in Shakespeare's hometown of Stratford. In many Christian churches, babies were **baptized** a few days after they were born. This meant that the minister said blessings for the baby and sprinkled water over him. The written records from the church tell us that a baby named William Shakspere was baptized at the church on April 26, 1564. "Shakspere" was another way of spelling "Shakespeare." William was probably born just a few days before that date in a house that belonged to his parents, John and Mary.

Shakespeare was probably born in this house.
Today, it's a museum.

The second clue is a document from
November 1582, when Shakespeare was 18 years
old.  It's a record of his marriage to a woman
named Anne Hathaway, who was 26 at the time
— eight years older than William.

Anne Hathaway grew up in this large farmhouse.

The third clue is from only six months later. It's a record of the baptism of Anne and William's first child, Susanna. Since the baby was baptized only six months after the wedding, Anne must have been about three months pregnant when she married William.

The fourth document is the record of another baptism in 1585. At this time, William and Anne became the parents of twins — a girl named Judith and a boy named Hamnet.

That's it. Between Shakespeare's birth and his early 20s, we have only four written records about his life. What happened between Shakespeare's birth and the birth of his children? We don't know for sure, but we can make some pretty good guesses because we know some things about life in England during Shakespeare's time.

## Shakespeare in School

As a boy, Shakespeare probably went to school in the town of Stratford. In Shakespeare's time, more people were becoming **literate** (able to read and write) than ever before in the history of England. More than 100 new schools were built in England around that time.

But even though more people were becoming literate, not all children went to school. Most parents were too poor to send their children to school. They needed their children to work to help support the family.

Shakespeare's father John wasn't wealthy, but he wasn't poor either. John was a successful businessman who bought and sold wool.

He was also a successful glove-maker. Eventually, he went on to become the town's mayor. Because Shakespeare's father had enough money, William probably would have been sent to school.

What was education like in those days? William would have started at the **petty school** (the school for young boys and girls) when he was four or five years old. After leaving the petty school, girls were educated at home, but boys could go on to **grammar school**.

Stratford's grammar school was on the upper floor of this building.

13

William would have stayed in grammar school until he was about 15 years old.

School started at six in the morning in summer, at seven in the morning in winter. The boys worked all day long, with a short break at lunchtime. They sat on long benches or stools with no desks and learned to write with feather pens that were dipped in ink.

Grammar school boys learned how to write with feather pens like this one.

If students didn't behave well, teachers sometimes hit them with wooden sticks as a punishment.

Some boys went on from grammar school to university, but Shakespeare never did. He may have left school to help his father in the family business.

## Shakespeare's Town in the English Countryside

Today in England, most people live in cities or big towns, but in Shakespeare's time, most people lived in small towns or villages. Back then, only 8 out of every 100 English people lived in a town of 5000 people or more. The rest of the people (about 92 out of every 100 people) lived in even smaller towns or on farms. Most people worked on the land as farmers.

Shakespeare's town of Stratford had only 1500 people, but it was busy for its size. Because Stratford was located on a road to the big city of London, many people stopped in Stratford when they were traveling to London.

In Shakespeare's time, this bridge was on the road to London.

Perhaps it was seeing these travelers that gave Shakespeare the idea of going to London himself someday.

Stratford was also busy because it was a market town. Every week, people from other nearby towns came into Stratford. They came to buy and sell food, animals, and other things that they had made or grown. Shakespeare's plays contain many words about flowers, birds, and animals. His work is full of the sights, sounds, and smells of life in a small country town.

## Chapter Summary

In this chapter, you learned some facts about the early life of William Shakespeare. Shakespeare grew up in a town called Stratford and got married at 18 to an older woman, Anne Hathaway, who was three months pregnant at the time. You read about schools in Shakespeare's time, and about the town of Stratford and the countryside where Shakespeare grew up.

In the next chapter, you'll read about the next years in Shakespeare's life, when he left the small town of Stratford and moved to the filthy, crowded city of London.

Chapter Two

# Shakespeare Comes to London

## Questions this chapter will answer:

- **Why was London growing during Shakespeare's time?**

- **Why was the River Thames so important to business in London?**

Nobody knows for sure how or when Shakespeare left Stratford and went to London, because, after 1585 when his twins were baptized, Shakespeare disappears for a while from the Stratford records.

He doesn't show up again in any documents until seven or eight years later. These seven or eight years are called the Lost Years because there is no record of what Shakespeare did during that time.

But around 1592 we find documents showing that Shakespeare was writing poems and plays in London and acting in London theatres.

Shakespeare experts have a theory about why he left Stratford. They believe that he may have decided to join a **company** (group) of actors. These companies traveled around the countryside to entertain the townspeople. Perhaps it was after one of these performances that Shakespeare decided to become an actor and a playwright.

Whatever the reason, at some point Shakespeare left Stratford and ended up in the city of London on the River Thames. During Shakespeare's time, London was becoming one of the most exciting and powerful cities in Europe.

## The Growing City of London

Shakespeare wasn't the only person to go to London during the 16th century. More than 100,000 other people moved there, too. Many of these people were country farmers who couldn't make a living as farmers any more, so they came to the city looking for work.

This is a map of London in the 16th century.

River Thames

The oldest part of London was on the north side of the River Thames.

Before reading further, take a look at the map. Can you see anything on it that shows that the city of London was growing? (Five white dots have been added to the map to show you where to look.)

On the north side of the river, there is a border of thick walls around the main part of town. These stone walls were built in ancient times to protect the city from attackers. Inside the walls was the heart of the ancient city of London. The ancient city wasn't very large. The walls were only about two miles long.

But the city was spreading out beyond its ancient center. Look at how many buildings there are outside the old city walls. The old heart of the city was too crowded, so people were beginning to build homes and other buildings outside the old walls. If you look at the edges of the map, you'll see that there was much more space outside the walls. The streets and houses were more spread out. You can see that there are trees and fields around them.

When Shakespeare arrived,
London was becoming crowded.

21

During the 1500s, the **population** of London grew fast. (The population of a place is all the people who live there.) In the 1520s, before Shakespeare was born, there had been no more than 60,000 residents in London. But only 80 years later, in 1600, there were 200,000 people living there. At this size, London was much bigger than any other English town. Other big towns in England had 25,000 people at the most.

## London's Busy River

After growing up in a small town like Stratford, Shakespeare must have been overwhelmed by all the action in London. He must have noticed how busy things were, especially along the river. The River Thames was bustling with traffic. Many different sorts of boats could be seen on the river. Some were small rowboats. Others were tall ships with three masts and many sails.

The smaller boats on the river were used for carrying people around London. There was only one bridge across the river, called London Bridge, so many people used **water taxis** to cross from one bank to another. Other water taxis carried people up and down the river. The men rowing the taxis called out "Westward ho!" or "Eastward ho!" to let passengers know which direction they would be heading. The larger boats and ships were used for transporting goods. Roads were bad in England in the 1500s, so the fastest way to move things around was by boat.

Ships like these transported goods from overseas.

Some of these boats were on the river because **industry** was growing in England during this time. (Industry means making things in factories.) In London, more and more factories were making goods for sale. The city was covered in smoke from these factories. Boats brought materials like wood, leather, coal, lead, copper, and tin from other parts of England. Workers in London used these materials to build ships and make many other products.

Trade with other countries was also growing during Shakespeare's time. (Trade means the business of buying and selling products.) Large ships brought goods from overseas to London's port — sugar, spices, nuts, figs, and wine. Some of these goods ended up being sold in town markets like the one in Stratford.

In Shakespeare's time, goods were shipped in packages like these.

London's port and river became busier and busier as trade increased between England and other countries in Europe. Trading companies were formed to import goods from other countries into England and to export English goods to other countries.

## Chapter Summary

In this chapter, you read that the city of London grew enormously during Shakespeare's time. The population of the city was 200,000 by the end of the 16th century. Many factories were built in London during Shakespeare's time, and the river became busier as industry and trade grew. Smaller boats carried people up, down, and across the river. Larger ships brought goods from other countries to be sold in England. They also carried English goods across the seas to be sold in other countries.

In the next chapter we'll take a closer look at what it was like for Shakespeare to live in London.

Chapter Three

# Filthy but Fun — Life in Shakespeare's London

**Questions this chapter will answer:**

• **What was it like to live in London in Shakespeare's time?**

• **Why did Londoners like to go outside the old city walls?**

Put yourself in Shakespeare's shoes. Imagine what it was like for him to see England's biggest and most crowded city for the first time.

From far away, Shakespeare would have seen thick gray smoke hanging in the air over the city. As he got closer, he would have smelled something terrible. People said that in those days, you could smell London from 20 miles away.

Why did London smell so bad? And was there anything about the city that people really enjoyed? You'll find out in this chapter.

A narrow street in London in the 1500s

## The Dirty Side of London

There were some wealthy people in London, but most of London's population was poor and lived in terrible conditions.

One writer in Shakespeare's time said that the buildings in London seemed to be "jostling one another" and trying to knock each other down. In the poorest parts of the city, buildings blocked out the sunlight, making the crowded streets dark and damp.

The streets of London weren't just crowded — they also smelled terrible. They smelled bad because they were flooded with human waste.

Today, most modern cities have underground **sewage systems**. The sewage system carries dirty water from toilets away from buildings to a place where it can be treated and disposed of. But in Shakespeare's time, London didn't have a real sewage system. Instead of toilets, people used pots in their bedrooms. These pots were called **chamber pots** (pots for the bedroom). People emptied their chamber pots into open ditches that ran along the middle of the street. Some of the ditches drained into the river. All this sewage everywhere made the city smell disgusting.

In Shakespeare's day, people dumped their toilet waste from a chamber pot like this into the street.

There were other reasons for the terrible smell, too. Animal waste and garbage were piled up in the streets. In the middle of the city there was a **slaughterhouse** (a place where animals are butchered). Blood from the slaughterhouse ran out into the streets. And in the fields outside the city, people dumped dead animals and left them to rot.

The water supply in London was another problem. People in London didn't have indoor plumbing. This meant that there were no pipes to bring water into homes.

Some people had water delivered to their homes in barrels or jugs from wells or fountains. Others went to the river or to other spots around the city to fill bottles with river water. But, as you have read, London's ditches dumped sewage into the river, so the river was a breeding ground for disease. The water made people sick. It also tasted bad because the tides carried salty seawater up the river.

The water supply improved in the early 1600s. A company called the New River Company dug a channel that was 40 miles long. This channel brought water into the London area from far outside the city.

## The Wild Life Outside the Ancient Walls

The parts of London that were outside the ancient walls were some of the roughest but most exciting parts of the city. This was where Londoners went to break the rules and to be entertained.

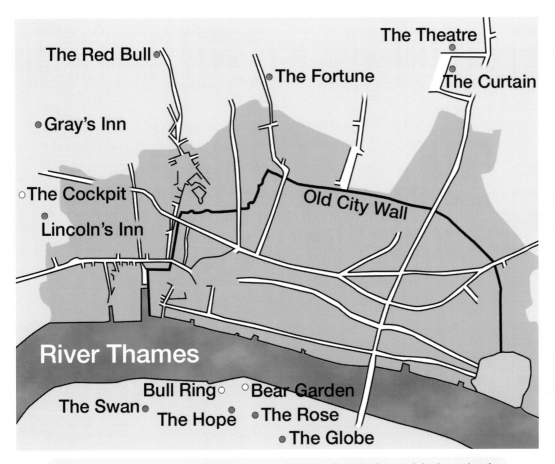

The red dots show where plays were performed outside London's ancient walls. The white dots show other types of fun.

City leaders had no control over the areas outside the ancient walls. In these areas, people could do things that were against the rules inside the walls. For example, inside the city walls, people were not allowed to set up brothels (buildings where prostitutes worked), so they set up brothels just outside the walls instead.

The dark and narrow streets in this outer part of London attracted thieves, especially **cutpurses**. A cutpurse was a kind of pickpocket. In those days, a man carried his money in a small bag called a purse that was tied to his belt with strings. Cutpurses would cut the strings and run off with the purse before the man realized that he had been robbed. Cutpurses were often young boys who worked in gangs. At one point, London even had a secret school for cutpurses, where boys learned how to steal.

There were many inns and taverns where people stopped to eat and drink. Many of them got drunk. One of Shakespeare's most famous characters was a man named Falstaff, a fat old fool who wasted most of his time at an inn, getting drunk and joking with his friends.

Falstaff living it up at an inn

Another reason that Londoners went outside the city walls was to watch cruel, bloody animal shows. One kind of show, which was called bear-baiting, took place in an arena named the Bear Garden.

In the Bear Garden, a bear was chained in the middle of a ring so that it couldn't escape. The crowds cheered as packs of large dogs called mastiffs entered the ring and attacked the bear. The crowds roared as the bear and the dogs tore each other to pieces.

Londoners loved watching bloody contests between dogs and bears.

34

At the spot where the Bear Garden used to be, the bones of bears and dogs have been found buried deep in the ground. Hazelnut shells have also been found. Today, at the movies, people eat popcorn, but in Shakespeare's times, people ate hazelnuts when they watched a show. The hazelnut shells on the ground soaked up blood. Maybe some of those shells were dropped by William Shakespeare himself. In one of his plays, he has an actor dress up as a bear and chase another actor off the stage. Maybe he got this idea from watching a show at the Bear Garden.

Bear-baiting wasn't the only kind of animal show people went to see. There were also bull-baiting shows. In these shows, a bull went up against bulldogs. Londoners also watched cockfights, which were fights between two roosters.

In the late 1500s, Londoners began to flock to see another kind of entertainment on the outskirts of the city — plays. The area just outside the city of London is the place where William Shakespeare's plays were first performed.

## Chapter Summary

In this chapter you learned more about what London was like during Shakespeare's time. London was dirty and smelly because the streets were filled with sewage.

The part of the city outside the ancient walls was a rough, wild area, where many Londoners went for entertainment like animal fights. Shakespeare almost certainly would have been one of the visitors to the wild part of the city. The area outside the ancient walls was also the place where many of the city's theatres were located. In the next chapter, you'll read about plays in London.

Chapter Four

# Pens, Swords, Plays, and Playwrights

**Questions this chapter will answer:**

- **What was it like to go and see a play in Shakespeare's time?**

- **What was it like to be a playwright?**

The rowdy audience whooped and hollered. A drunken man slurped his beer. Women walked around selling apples. Young lads threw rotten fruit and munched on nuts. Cutpurses worked the crowd, stealing money when nobody was looking.

Up in the top balcony, prostitutes fluttered their handkerchiefs, hoping that men would notice them and decide to pay them a visit. Believe it or not, this was the scene at London's theatres in the 1500s.

37

After he arrived in London, Shakespeare became a part of the theatre world. He probably joined a theatre company and started out as an actor before beginning to write plays. Eventually, he became a big success, writing a string of plays that wowed the London crowds.

The Globe theatre was first built during Shakespeare's time. It was rebuilt not too long ago. If you're ever in London, you can go and see a play there.

The country boy from Stratford was making a name for himself in the big city.

This chapter takes a closer look at the wild and crazy world of the theatre in London.

Today, inside the rebuilt Globe, you can see a play being performed the way it was done in Shakespeare's time.

## Going to See a Play

Imagine being a Londoner in Shakespeare's day. If you wanted to see a play at the Globe theatre, you'd first look across the river to make sure that the theatre's flag was flying. If it was, you knew that a play was going to be performed there that afternoon.

39

People from all walks of life went to the theatre. Wealthy Londoners came from their mansions on the north bank of the river to watch plays from the more expensive balcony seats. Poor Londoners paid a penny to stand in front of the stage. Rich Londoners sometimes called these people "groundlings," because they stood on the ground, or called them "stinkards," because they smelled bad. Crowds came to the theatre to be entertained. The actors and the playwright worked hard to wow the audience with special effects. Stages had trapdoors and ropes so that actors could appear and disappear suddenly.

In this scene from *Hamlet*, the hole below the trapdoor is a grave.

The roof of the Globe was made of thatch (straw).  In some plays at the Globe, the actors shot off a cannon as a special effect.  Once, at a play in 1613, a shot from the cannon caught the roof on fire and the whole theatre burned to the ground.  It was rebuilt in 1614 with a tile roof.

Crowds at the Globe liked to see blood and guts on the stage.  If a play had a stabbing scene, the actors used a special knife with a hollow handle.  When the knife was jammed against an actor's chest, it would look like the character was being stabbed, but in fact the blade of the knife wouldn't go into the actor's body — it would slide back into the handle of the knife.

Actors used sheep's blood to make violent scenes seem more real.  The blood was stored under the actor's clothes in an animal bladder (the inside part of an animal where urine is collected).  When the blade of the knife touched the bladder, it would burst and the blood would run all over the stage.

In one play, the actors used the heart, lungs, and liver of a dead sheep to make a scene bloodier and more realistic for the audience.  In another play, a character had his head cut off.  For this trick, the actors used a fake head that was filled with a bladder of blood.  The blood poured all over the stage during the scene.

Swords and fighting have always
been popular in Shakespeare's plays.

The companies spent a lot of money on
costumes to impress the audience. These
costumes were especially important for the
female characters because female characters
were always played by men and boys. Females
were not allowed on the stage. The costumes
and makeup helped the audience forget that
all the actors were really male.

## Playwrights with Pens and Swords

When you think of a playwright in the 1500s, you might imagine a serious young man writing quietly in a candle-lit room. In truth, the world of the actors and playwrights was sometimes wild and dangerous, full of competition and jealousy.

All the playwrights wore swords on their belts, and they used them. During Shakespeare's time, a number of playwrights and actors killed other men in **duels** with swords. (A duel is a fight between two people, using swords or guns.)

This famous playwright, Ben Jonson, killed an actor in a swordfighting duel.

Other playwrights and actors were killed in duels themselves. One famous playwright, Christopher Marlowe, died after being stabbed in the eye in a fight at a tavern late one afternoon.

This is a scene from a Marlowe play. His plays were violent, like his life.

At first, Shakespeare may have felt like an outsider among some of the London playwrights. Marlowe had been part of a group of playwrights that was known as "the University Wits" because they had all been students at a university. (A wit is a person who makes good jokes.) This group probably looked down on Shakespeare, who had never gone to university.

Shakespeare may have felt like an outsider, but he made a place for himself. He was known as a speedy writer. Another playwright said that Shakespeare "never blotted out a line." He probably meant that Shakespeare was sure of himself and didn't have to go back to fix mistakes.

Being a quick writer would have helped Shakespeare to become a success. Today, actors may **rehearse** (practice) for weeks or months, and they may perform the same play for many weeks or months in a row. In Shakespeare's time, the crowds were always demanding new plays. Companies performed as many as 15 different plays in one month. The playwrights were busy men, cranking out new plays all the time.

© North Wind Picture Archives

Some people today believe that Shakespeare wrote very quickly. Others are not so sure.

## Chapter Summary

In this chapter, you read about the world of the theatre in London and learned what it was like to go and see a play in Shakespeare's time. The audience was loud and rowdy, and the actors used special effects to wow the audience. Playwrights led very busy lives and got into plenty of trouble. A few of the playwrights and actors were killed in duels, or else killed other people.

In the next chapter, you'll read about why the theatres were all shut down in 1592 and 1593.

Chapter Five

# "Bring out Your Dead"

**Questions this chapter will answer:**

• **What was it like to die of the disease called the plague?**

• **How did people try to keep the plague from spreading?**

• **What was the cause of the plague?**

The year is 1593, and these are terrible times in London.

A man leads a horse-drawn cart along a dark and narrow street. "Bring out your dead!" he cries.

"God save us!" sobs a woman in a nearby house. "Have mercy on us!"

Seeing a dark lump on the road, the man stops the cart. It's another dead body, lying face down in the muck. The man drags the body into the cart, flipping it onto a pile of corpses that keeps growing and growing.

This chapter is about the disease that killed all these people, including one of Shakespeare's own brothers.

Why are these men smoking as they load bodies onto a cart? You will find out later in the chapter.

## A Killer Disease

A terrible disease called the plague swept through London between 1592 and 1594, when about 125,000 people lived there. It killed more than 11,000 people. That was one out of every ten Londoners.

Victims of the plague died a painful death, with bad fevers, stomach aches, and vomiting. Victims got red or black lumps the size of apples in their groins and under their armpits. These painful swellings were called buboes. The plague was called **bubonic plague** because of the buboes.

The bubonic plague moved quickly. When people got the disease, they often died within a few days. An Italian writer said that people with the plague "ate lunch with their friends and dinner with their ancestors in paradise." He meant that if you caught the plague, you might feel fine at lunchtime, but by dinnertime you could be dead.

A Start-to-Finish author visits the bones of plague victims in France. Bubonic plague killed millions of people in Europe.

Doctors tried to cure the sick. Their treatments seem odd to us today, but in Shakespeare's time, people thought they might work. One treatment was to open and drain the swollen buboes with a pointed metal rod. After heating the rod in a fire, the doctor drove its heated point into the buboes in the victim's groin and armpits.

Doctors used a hot metal rod like this to open buboes.

Some healers tried to treat the plague by roasting whole onions and then placing them on the buboes. Other healers plucked the tail feathers off a pigeon and then pressed the pigeon's rear end onto the victim's buboes. This was supposed to suck the sickness out.

## Trying to Keep the Plague from Spreading

Londoners were terrified of the plague. They had all sorts of ways of trying to avoid getting the disease.

Some people carried lucky charms, called **amulets**. They believed that amulets had the power to ward off the plague.

Some people thought that strong smells would save them from the disease. They burned herbs, leather, and even feces to create strong smells in their houses. Others kept smelly goats inside their homes. When walking along the street, men smoked pipes and wealthy women would swing a pomander in front of them. A pomander was a small container that the women filled with strong-smelling herbs.

51

Some women carried pomanders like this one. They filled them with herbs, believing that the smell would keep the plague away.

London's city leaders knew that the disease was very **contagious**. (This means that the disease could quickly pass from person to person.) But people didn't really know *how* it spread. To try to keep it from spreading, they closed down the theatres, taverns, and other places where people gathered together in crowds. They wouldn't even allow people to have funerals for dead relatives.

City leaders also made other rules to try to keep the plague from spreading. If somebody in your household became sick, you and your family were put under **quarantine**. In those days, quarantine meant being separated from other people for forty days. Nobody in the house was allowed to go out, and the doors and windows were sometimes nailed shut to keep all the people inside. A cross was painted on the door to warn people on the outside to stay away.

## A Cause That No One Understood

People in Shakespeare's time didn't know it, but the plague was actually spread by fleas. The fleas carried invisible germs called **bacteria**. When the fleas bit people and sucked out their blood, the fleas also passed the plague bacteria into the people's bodies, and those people soon became sick with the plague.

People in Shakespeare's time didn't know that the plague was spread by fleas like this one.

But the plague bacteria had another home besides the fleas. That home was inside the bodies of black rats. Rats roamed the dirty streets of London, feeding on piles of rotting garbage. The rats carried the plague germs with them, and the fleas lived most of the time on the rats. When rats died of plague, fleas moved to humans, spreading the germs from rats to people.

54

The fleas that spread the plague lived on black rats like this one. The rats spread the fleas all around London.

The plague spread quickly because London was so crowded. With rats and people jammed together, fleas jumped easily from rat to rat or from person to person. The plague killed rich people and poor people, but it spread most quickly and killed the most people in the poorest, most crowded areas of the city.

Londoners were so afraid of the disease that they left the city if they possibly could. Wealthy Londoners went away to their country homes. The theatres were closed, so companies of actors, probably including Shakespeare, left London and performed in other places. Many people did escape the plague by leaving the city, but others carried the disease with them and spread it to people in the countryside and other English towns.

William Shakespeare never caught the plague, but at least one of his younger brothers did, and maybe two. We know that Shakespeare's brother Gilbert caught the plague, and he was lucky enough to survive. William's youngest brother, Edmund, who was also an actor, died in London in 1607, at the age of 27. Since this was the time when a second round of the plague was hitting London, it seems likely that Edmund died of the plague. This photo shows the church in London where William helped to bury Edmund.

This is where William's brother Edmund was buried in 1607, in a part of London called Bankside.

## Chapter Summary

In this chapter, you learned about the bubonic plague. The chapter explained what it was like to suffer from this disease. Doctors didn't know that the disease was spread by fleas that lived on rats. They tried to treat it and keep it from spreading, but they couldn't. The disease killed more than 11,000 people in London in the early 1590s. Now, if you think death from the plague was bad, try reading the next chapter, all about crime and punishment in Shakespeare's England.

## Chapter Six

# Crime and Punishment

**Questions this chapter will answer:**

• **How were crimes punished in Shakespeare's day?**

• **How were traitors punished?**

You've already read about the theatre and bear-baiting in Shakespeare's London, but there was another form of entertainment in the city that really brought out the crowds — hangings, whippings and other bloody punishments. Londoners loved to watch people being punished for breaking the law.

Londoners came out in crowds
to watch criminals being punished.

Just like at the theatre, the audiences ate
snacks of fruit or nuts while they were watching
the punishments.  Some **offenders** (people who
had committed crimes) were allowed to make
speeches before their punishments.  The crowds
listened to the speeches as if they were listening
to a play in the theatre.  They cheered if they
liked a speech and they booed if they didn't.

In some towns and villages in England,
the punishments took place on market days
so that the crowds would be as big as possible.

People saw the punishments when they came to the market to buy food or other things they needed.

In London, people went to different parts of the city to see different kinds of punishments. If people wanted to watch a **beheading** (a person's head being chopped off) they went to one place.

On this spot, behind the walls of the Tower of London, Queen Elizabeth had one of her nobles beheaded in 1601.

If they wanted to watch a hanging, they went to another place.

In this chapter, you'll read about crime and punishment on the streets of London in Shakespeare's time. As you read, imagine crowds of hundreds and even thousands of people coming out to watch.

## Punishing Crimes

Most people who had committed crimes were not punished with jail time. Some of their punishments were much worse.

For small crimes, the offender was punished with public embarrassment. Some offenders were placed in a cart or tied facing backward on a horse and then they were led past jeering crowds. (Jeering means yelling rude and insulting things at someone.)

Sometimes offenders were placed in wooden **stocks**. The stocks were clamped around the prisoners' ankles so that the prisoners couldn't move. The prisoners had to hold signs that described their crimes, and crowds would gather around to jeer at them.

For more severe crimes, the offenders were placed in the **pillory**. We say they were pilloried. The pillory was like the stocks, but it was locked around the prisoner's neck and wrists instead of the ankles.

This meant that offenders couldn't dodge out of the way when people in the crowd threw stones, vegetables, or even dead animals at their heads.

A pillory was locked around the offender's neck and wrists.

Some pilloried offenders were actually struck in the head and killed by objects that were thrown by the crowd. Some offenders were whipped.

Another type of punishment was **maiming**. Maiming means cutting off or destroying some part of the body.

One London servant girl was pilloried and had her ears cut off for trying to poison her master. A London man was pilloried twice after he tried to arrange to have somebody murdered. Each time that he was locked into the pillory, one of his ears was cut off.

Some offenders had one of their hands cut off. Or sometimes the offender was branded with a hot iron. This means that a red-hot metal tool was pressed against the offender's skin. The iron burned the skin and left a scar that would never go away. If the crime was stealing, the offender might be branded with a "T" for "Thief."

## Punishing Traitors

One of the very worst punishments was for the crime of **treason**. Today, treason means a crime against your own country. In Shakespeare's time, treason meant a crime against the king or queen. Somebody who commits treason is called a **traitor**.

For most of Shakespeare's life, Elizabeth was the Queen of England. In fact, Shakespeare's time is called the Elizabethan Age. Under Elizabeth's rule, traitors were killed by being hanged, drawn, and quartered. This was a long and horrible way to die. The person in charge of the killing was called the **executioner**.

Being drawn meant that the traitor was tied to a wooden frame and dragged through the streets to the place where he would be executed. Then he was hanged by the neck until he was *almost* dead. The people wanted him to be alive for the rest of the punishment. The executioner then cut the traitor down from the rope for the next torture.

After the hanging, while the traitor was still alive, the executioner cut open the traitor's abdomen (the front of his body, below his ribs and above his legs). The executioner then pulled out the traitor's internal organs. If the traitor was lucky, he fainted or passed out before his heart was cut out of his body. But sometimes he was still conscious and knew what was happening to him right up to the end.

Although the traitor was now dead, the punishment still wasn't over. The traitor's intestines and heart were burned, and his body was divided into four quarters. Each of the traitor's four body parts was taken to a different part of the city and put on display as a warning. The bloody head was stuck on the top of a pole, and placed on London Bridge. The head was an ugly warning to the people of London not to be a traitor to the king or queen.

Elizabeth I was queen of England during much of Shakespeare's life. Although she was hard on traitors, she was a big fan of Shakespeare's plays.

As you read earlier, there was a lot of violence in theatre in Shakespeare's time. And there is a lot of violence in many of Shakespeare's own plays. With so much violent punishment for people to see for free on the streets, the theatres probably had to be violent, too, in order to attract big audiences.

You can still visit the Tower of London, where many traitors were tortured and killed.

## Chapter Summary

In this chapter, you read about how crimes were punished in Shakespeare's time. Some criminals were placed on carts, or horses, or in stocks and pillories in front of jeering crowds. Some offenders were maimed. Their ears or hands were cut off or they were branded with a hot branding iron.

The bloodiest punishment was the one for traitors. After they were hanged, the bodies of traitors were cut open and their intestines and hearts were pulled out. Then they were cut into pieces and the pieces were displayed around London as a warning.

The next chapter is a happier one about the mystery and greatness of Shakespeare's plays.

Chapter Seven

# Shakespeare for All Time

## Questions this chapter will answer:

- **Why do some people think that Shakespeare didn't write the plays?**

- **Why does Shakespeare still matter today?**

By 1600, the turn of the new century, Shakespeare was at the top of his game. He wrote some of his most famous plays around this time, including *Hamlet*, *Othello*, *King Lear*, and *Macbeth*. His company pulled in huge audiences from all around London and from overseas. As co-owner of the Globe theatre, Shakespeare became a rich man.

Students tour the inside of the Globe theatre today.

Becoming rich allowed Shakespeare to buy land back in Stratford. He had left his hometown many years before, but his wife and daughters were still there. His son, Hamnet, had died at the age of 11. Shakespeare still visited his family there and must have felt attached to the place.

After 1610, Shakespeare didn't write much any more. He may have stayed around London for a few more years, giving advice to the new up-and-coming writers in the company.

Nobody knows exactly when Shakespeare returned to his hometown, but he lived out his last days in Stratford with his wife, Anne. He died in April 1616.

In this chapter, you'll read about what people have said about Shakespeare's plays since his death.

## Did Shakespeare Really Write the Plays?

Most scholars believe that as a playwright, William Shakespeare could do it all. He wrote about 37 plays. He wrote about love and passion in *Romeo and Juliet*. He wrote comedies, like *A Midsummer Night's Dream*. He wrote dark tragedies, like *Hamlet*. He wrote ancient histories, like *Julius Caesar*. He wrote plays set in ancient Rome, in Italy, and in France. Experts agree that only a person with enormous talent could have done all this.

But some scholars think that William Shakespeare from Stratford wasn't the man with all that talent. They think that he didn't have a good enough education to have written all the plays. They think that somebody else wrote them and published them under the **pen name** of William Shakespeare. Pen names are names that some writers use in order to keep their real names secret.

These scholars believe that only a very well-educated man could have written plays filled with so much knowledge of history, law, foreign countries, and ancient writings. There is no evidence that Shakespeare had that kind of education. Many of these scholars believe that the plays were secretly written by a man called the Earl of Oxford.

The Tragicall Historie of

# HAMLET
Prince of Denmarke.

*Enter two Centinels.*

1. STand: who is that?
2. STis I.
1. O you come most carefully vpon your watch,
2. And if you meete *Marcellus* and *Horatio*,
The partners of my watch, bid them make haste.
1. I will: See who goes there.
*Enter Horatio and Marcellus.*
*Hor.* Friends to this ground.
*Mar.* And leegemen to the Dane,
O farewell honest souldier, who hath releeued you?
1. *Barnardo* hath my place, giue you good night.
*Mar.* Holla, *Barnardo.*
2. Say, is *Horatio* there?
*Hor.* A peece of him.
2. Welcome *Horatio*, welcome good *Marcellus.*
*Mar.* What hath this thing appear'd againe to night.
2. I haue seene nothing.
*Mar.* *Horatio* sayes tis but our fantasie,
And wil not let beliefe take hold of him,
Touching this dreaded sight twice seene by v,

© North Wind Picture Archives

Shakespeare wrote plays that took place in many different lands. *Hamlet* was set in the kingdom of Denmark.

For this reason, they call themselves Oxfordians. The Earl of Oxford was wealthy and educated. He traveled to other countries and had a huge library of books.

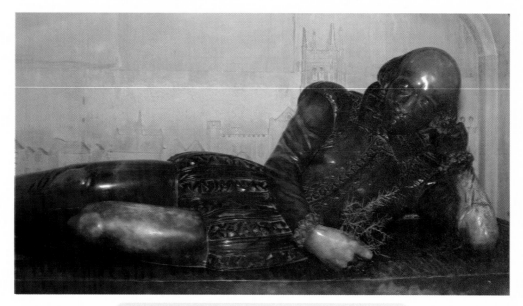

This is said to be William Shakespeare. But did this man really write all the plays?

Most Shakespeare experts think that William Shakespeare *did* write most of the plays. These scholars call themselves "Stratfordians" to show their support for the man from Stratford. They say, "Shakespeare got a good education at the local grammar school, and his genius took him the rest of the way."

Some scholars think that the Earl of Oxford
is the real author of Shakespeare's plays.

"Then why aren't there more written records
to show that Shakespeare really was a playwright
and not just an actor?" the Oxfordians ask.
"While Shakespeare was alive, no one seems
to have written a single letter that mentions
his playwriting."

The Stratfordians answer, "How do you
know?  Many old documents about Shakespeare
may have been lost."

Today, most scholars continue to believe that
William Shakespeare of Stratford wrote most of
the plays.  But the debate goes on.  Unless more
old records or documents are found, we may
never know for sure.

## A Writer for All Time

"He was not of an age, but for all time!"
The famous playwright Ben Jonson wrote these
words about his friend, William Shakespeare.
He meant that Shakespeare wasn't just a popular
writer of his own time. His greatness would
last forever.

So far, Jonson's words have turned out
to be true. Shakespeare's plays are still read
and performed today, 400 years after he died.
They have been performed in just about every
language. Thousands of books have been
written about them. In 1983, somebody put
together a list of all the books that have been
written about just one of Shakespeare's plays,
*Henry V*. There were 2000 books on the list!
In recent times, many of Shakespeare's plays
have been made into movies.

In this scene from *Hamlet*, Prince Hamlet
jokes about death.

Why are Shakespeare's works still so interesting to people all around the world? It's because the ideas and feelings in the plays are timeless. The plays are filled with love, action, comedy, murder, death, and war. The characters in Shakespeare's plays are still real to us today. Lovers understand the passion of Romeo and Juliet. Many young people relate to the angry and tormented young Hamlet.

An Italian painter painted this scene in 1823. He called it "The Last Kiss of Romeo and Juliet."

Shakespeare's works are also important because they helped to create the English language that we speak today. Around 1500 of the words we use today were seen first in William Shakespeare's writings. He may have invented them himself, or he may have heard them spoken and decided to put them into his plays and poems. And even if he didn't actually invent the words, he helped to make them a common part of the English language. *Eyeball*, *hint*, *puppy dog*, *excellent*, and *lonely* — these are just some of the words that appeared for the first time in Shakespeare's writings. Each time you say these words you are speaking Shakespeare's English.

Many of the expressions that we use were invented by Shakespeare. If you tell somebody that your old bike has "seen better days," you are using a phrase that Shakespeare made up. The next time you hear somebody say that a person is "fair game," you'll know that those are Shakespeare's words as well.

## Chapter Summary

In this chapter you read that, by the end of his career, Shakespeare was rich and famous as one of England's best playwrights. He eventually retired to Stratford and died there in 1616.

Some scholars don't believe that Shakespeare from Stratford wrote all the plays and poems that have his name on them. Oxfordians think that these works were mostly written by the Earl of Oxford. But most Shakespeare experts don't agree. They say that the man from Stratford wrote the plays himself.

William Shakespeare is still important today, about 400 years after his death. When Shakespeare was growing up in Stratford, did anybody imagine that he would one day move to London and become the most famous name in the history of theatre? Probably not, but that is what he did. And, along the way, he gave us many of the words we speak today. Shakespeare's plays are still being read, performed, and loved around the world.

# Glossary

| Word | Definition | Page |
|------|-----------|------|
| amulet | an object that people carried to bring good luck<br>Some people thought that an amulet could keep them from getting sick. | 51 |
| bacteria | invisible germs that can make people sick | 53 |
| baptize | In the Christian church, some babies are baptized. This means that a priest or minister says blessings for the baby and sprinkles the baby with water. | 9 |
| behead | to cut a person's head off | 60 |
| bubonic plague | a disease that killed many thousands of people during Shakespeare's time | 49 |
| chamber pot | a pot that people used as a toilet in their bedrooms | 28 |
| contagious | If a disease can pass quickly from one person to another, we say that it is contagious. | 52 |
| company | a group of actors | 19 |
| cutpurse | a kind of pickpocket | 32 |

| Word | Definition | Page |
|---|---|---|
| duel | a fight between two people, using swords or guns | 43 |
| executioner | the person in charge of killing somebody who is being punished for a crime | 63 |
| grammar school | a school that some boys in England went to, in Shakespeare's time, after finishing **petty school** | 13 |
| industry | making things in factories | 23 |
| literate | able to read and write | 12 |
| maiming | cutting off or destroying a part of the body | 62 |
| offenders | people who have committed crimes | 59 |
| pen name | a name that a writer uses to keep his or her real name a secret | 71 |
| petty school | a school for young boys and girls in England in Shakespeare's time | 13 |

| Word | Definition | Page |
|------|-----------|------|
| pillory | a wooden frame that was used for punishing people during Shakespeare's time<br>A pillory was locked around a person's neck and wrists. | 61 |
| playwright | a person who writes a play | 5 |
| population | all the people who live in a place | 22 |
| quarantine | being kept away from other people for forty days | 53 |
| rehearse | to practice | 45 |
| sewage system | pipes or tunnels that carry dirty toilet water away from buildings to a place where it can be treated and disposed of | 28 |
| slaughterhouse | a place where animals are butchered | 29 |
| stocks | a wooden frame used for punishing people<br>The stocks were locked around a person's ankles. | 61 |
| trade | the business of buying and selling products | 24 |

| Word | Definition | Page |
|------|-----------|------|
| traitor | Someone who committed a crime against his own king or queen was called a traitor. | 63 |
| treason | a crime against a person's own country, king, or queen | 63 |
| | | 22 |
| water taxis | boats that took people across the river or up and down the river | |

## About the Author

Helen Sillett was born in England and lived in the Netherlands and Canada before moving to California as a teenager. She has taught history and literature classes to college students, and reading and writing classes to young adults. She is a writer and editor and has been a member of the Start-to-Finish team for several years.

Helen lives with her husband and their dog, Ella, in Los Angeles.

## About the Narrator

Nick Sandys has performed in theaters in Chicago, New York, Dallas, London, England, and Edinburgh, Scotland. You may also have heard Nick's voice in a television or radio commercial.

Nick works as a fight director helping actors make their fights look real on the stage. He also has a Master's degree in English Literature and has gone back to college to get a higher degree, called a PhD. He grew up in the ancient city of York, in the north of England.

# A Note to the Teacher

Start-to-Finish Core Content books are designed to help students achieve success in reading to learn. From the provocative cover question to the carefully structured and considerate text, these books promote inquiry, active engagement, and understanding. Not only do students learn curriculum-relevant content, but they learn how to read with understanding. Here are some of the features that make these books such powerful aids in teaching and learning.

## Structure That Supports Inquiry and Understanding

Core Content books are carefully structured to encourage students to ask questions, identify main ideas, and understand how ideas relate to one another. The structural features of the Blue Core Content books include the following:

- **"Introduction":** A concise introduction engages students in the book's topic and explicitly states the book's themes.
- **Clearly focused chapters:** Each of the following chapters focuses on a single topic at a length that makes for a comfortable session of reading.
- **"Questions This Chapter Will Answer":** Provocative questions following the chapter title reflect the chapter's main ideas. Each question corresponds to a heading within the chapter.
- **Chapter introduction:** An engaging opening leads to a clear statement of the chapter topic.
- **Carefully worded headings:** The headings within each chapter are carefully worded to signal the main idea of the section and reflect the opening questions.
- **Clear topic statements:** Within each chapter section, the main idea is explicitly stated so that students can distinguish it from supporting details.
- **"Chapter Summary":** A brief summary recaptures the main ideas signaled by the opening questions, text headings, and topic statements.

## Text That Is Written for Success™

Every page of a Core Content book is the product of a skilled team of educators, writers, and editors who understand your students' needs. The text features of these books include the following:

- **Mature treatment of grade level curriculum:** Core Content is age and grade-appropriate for the older student who is actively acquiring reading skills. The books also contain information that may be new to any student in the class, empowering Core Content readers to contribute interesting information to class discussions.
- **Idioms and vocabulary:** The text limits the density of new vocabulary and carefully introduces new words, new meanings of familiar words, and idioms. New subject-specific terms are bold-faced and included in the Glossary.
- **Background knowledge:** The text assumes little prior knowledge and anchors the reader using familiar examples and analogies.
- **Sentence structure:** Blue level text introduces a greater variety of complex sentences than are used at the easier Gold level to help students make a transition to the language of traditional textbooks.

## For More Information

To find out more about Start-to-Finish Core Content, visit www.donjohnston.com for full product information, standards and research base.